Exile Meditations

GABRIEL JACKSON

for SATB soloists or choir unaccompanied

MUSIC DEPARTMENT

OXFORD
UNIVERSITY PRESS

Commissioned by Christopher Walsh Sinka with the generous support of
the Portland State University Department of Music (Ethan Sperry, Director
of Choral Activities), the Latvian Relief Society of Canada (Daugavas Vanagi),
and the following individual donors: Andris Bankovskis, Beth Ann Beck,
Mārtiņš Bruveris, Lennie Cottrell, Ed Frazier Davis, Teresa Dragonetti, Paul French,
Māris Graudiņš, Evan Hirsch, Bob Iofis, Linda Jakobsone, Bill Keaton, Egils Levits,
Anna Marasco, Brendan Monte, Inese Nielsen, Alison Piasecka, Charlie Poe,
Bart Pushaw, Gunta Reynolds, Andrejs Ritiņš, David Rothzeid, Susan Saunders,
Solveiga Silkalna, Anna Sinka, Aivars and Nicola Sinka, Maija Sinka,
Gilbert Spencer, Jeff and Denise Walsh, and Ģirts and Velga Zēgners.

First performed by Agnese Urka (soprano), Dārta Treija (alto),
Christopher Walsh Sinka (tenor), and Eduards Fiskovičs (bass) at the Latvian
Railway History Museum, Riga, on 30 July 2017.

Duration: 29 minutes

Soprano—also plays Brake Drum
Tenor—also plays Claves
Bass—also plays Railwayman's Whistle

If the piece is performed by SATB choir, then one singer from S, T, and B will also
be required to play the minimal percussion parts.

TEXTS AND TRANSLATIONS

1.

Tās ilgas pēc dzimtenes brīvās,	*That yearning for your free homeland,*
Pēc zudušās mīļās un baltās,	*Dear, precious and lost,*
Tās nevar izrunāt vārdos,	*It cannot be put into words,*
Tās nevar izdziedāt dziesmās,	*It cannot be turned into song,*
Tās var vien izsāpēt, izsmelgt,	*It can only be lived through in pain,*
Tās klusi var izjust, var izciest	*It can only be quietly felt and endured*
No stundas uz stundu lēnām,	*Hour after hour, slowly,*
No dienas uz dienu lēnām,	*Day after day, slowly,*
No gada uz gadu lēnām	*Year after year, slowly*
Un līdzi ņemt kapā vai urnā.	*And then taken with you to the urn or the grave.*

Pēteris Ērmanis (1893–1969)
(English translation by Rita Ruduša)

2.

We journey towards a home not of our flesh. Its chestnut trees are not of our bones.
Its rocks are not like goats in the mountain hymn. The pebbles' eyes are not lilies
We journey towards a home that does not halo our heads with a special sun.
Mythical women applaud us. A sea for us, a sea against us.
When water and wheat are not at hand, eat our love and drink our tears...
There are mourning scarves for poets. A row of marble statues will lift our voice.
And an urn to keep the dust of time away from our souls. Roses for us and against us.
You have your glory, we have ours. Of our home we see only the unseen: our mystery.
Glory is ours: a throne carried on feet torn by roads that led to every home but our own!
The soul must recognize itself in its very soul, or die here.

Mahmoud Darwish (1941–2008)

3.

Nav sava kapa,	*No grave of your own,*
nav sava krusta.	*No cross of your own.*
Nav pat sava vārda…	*Not even a name...*
It kā tu nebūtu	*As if you had neither*
dzimis, ne miris.	*been born nor died.*
Tik ūpji mēdās,	*Only owls cry mockingly,*
maitu putni kraukļi	*Ravens, scavenger birds*
biezokņos tumšos.	*In the dark woods.*
Gaudo tik vilki	*Only wolves howl*
puteņu naktīs.	*In winter blizzard.*
Kāpj kāvi debesīs	*Northern lights rise skyward*
liesmainos mēteļos.	*In their fiery cloaks,*
Meklē tavu kapu,	*Searching for your grave,*
meklē tavu vārdu.	*Searching for your name.*
Nevar atrast.	*Not finding one.*

Rūta Skujiņa (1907–64)
(English translation by Rita Ruduša)

4.

The night became long and the dark increased,
but I didn't find starlight to indicate the path.
The trip became long, and my footsteps began
to disappear, without them how would I find a way back...
I doze off with a dream petting my eyeball.
At the same time I fear the daybreak will bury me.
Don't ask about me.
Don't ask who I am.

Ammar Tabbab (b. 1984)

5.

Ir miljons mūs, ko pazīst daudzi,
Kā kailus burtus – D un P.
Mūs iztrenca kā bišu draudzi,
Kad stropu dūmiem izsvēpē.
    Mums nav vairs cerības nevienas,
    Tik pārtiekam no vakardienas.

Tur ungārs ugunīgs no Pustas,
Tur polis mieru neatrod.
Te latvietis kā ēna kustas,
Lūdz Dievam: manu zemi dod!
    Nav gan vairs cerības nevienas,
    Mums jāpārtiek no vakardienas.

Skumst brālis lietuvis no Kaunas,
Met čukstot krustu ukrainis.
Lai atkal noautos, drūms aunas
Ik rītu mājup igaunis.
    Bet nav vairs cerības nevienas,
    Tik jāpārtiek no vakardienas.

No gada gadā rieciens plānāks,
Bet augumā aug izsalkums.
Jau gaidām sen, kad, "lielie" sanāks
Un nolaupīto atdos mums.
    Āi, nav vairs cerības nevienas,
    Lemts pārtikt mums no vakardienas.

A million there, albeit for many, we go
By simply D and P.
Akin to family made homeless,
Smoked out from our hive of bees.
    We have no ray of hope today,
    And living off our yesterday.

A hot Hungarian is here from Puszta,
A Pole who finds no peace.
A Latvian walks shadow-like, praying,
Give me my land back, please!
    We truly have no hope today,
    And have to live off yesterday.

A Lithuanian, from Kaunas, forlorn,
A Ukrainian, whispering, crosses his heart.
An Estonian is homeward bound each morning,
Only to take his shoes off, every night.
    But we have no hope left today,
    And only live off yesterday.

From year to year the slice gets thinner,
While our hunger swells and grows.
For long we've waited: "Big Ones", gather
And give us back our stolen shores.
    Oh, not a ray of hope today,
    We're meant to live off yesterday.

Teodors Zeltiņš (1914–91)
(English translation by Rita Ruduša)

6.

Earth is pressing against us, trapping us in the final passage.
To pass through, we pull off our limbs.
Earth is squeezing us. If only we were its wheat, we might die and yet live.
If only it were our mother so that she might temper us with mercy.
If only we were pictures of rocks held in our dreams like mirrors.
We glimpse faces in their final battle for the soul, of those who will be killed
by the last living among us. We mourn their children's feast.
We saw the faces of those who would throw our children out of the windows
of this last space. A star to burnish our mirrors.
Where should we go after the last border? Where should birds fly after the last sky?
Where should plants sleep after the last breath of air?
We write our names with crimson mist!
We end the hymn with our flesh.
Here we will die. Here, in the final passage.
Here or there, our blood will plant olive trees.

Mahmoud Darwish (1941–2008)

7.

Tur, savā zemē, bij man sava sēta,	*There, in my homeland, I had a homestead.*
To atstāju es bargā likteņvarā,	*I left it in the hands of cruel fate,*
Kaut mani dēli gāja par to karā—	*Even if my sons had gone to war for it—*
Tā audžu audzēm bija svēta.	* Even if, for generations, it had been sacred.*
Tik vien es līdzi aiznesu no mājas	*All I had brought with me from home*
Kā sauju zemes. Kaisiet to pār šķirstu	*Is a handful of soil. Scatter it over my coffin,*
Man kapā, kad es svešā zemē mirstu—	*In the grave in a foreign land when I die—*
Lai tā pār maniem pīšļiem klājas.	* Let it cover my remains.*

Kārlis Dzilleja (1891–1963)
(English translation by Rita Ruduša)

LATVIAN PRONUNCIATION GUIDE

ā = long 'a' as in h**a**rd

ē = long 'a' as in m**a**de

ī = 'ee' as in s**ee**

o = 'oer' as in d**oer**

u = 'oo' as in f**oo**t

ū = 'oo' as in f**oo**d

ie = 'ie' as in happ**ie**r

ai = 'i' as in m**i**ne

au = 'ow' as in c**ow**

c = 'ts' as in ha**ts**

č = 'ch' as in **ch**ess

g = hard 'g' as in **g**arment

j = 'y' as in **y**ellow

k = hard 'c' as in **c**ard

ķ = 'ty' as in Ka**ty**a

ļ = 'll' as in mi**ll**ion

ņ = 'ny' as in ca**ny**on

r = rolled 'r'

s = 'c' as in **c**ity

š = 'sh' as in **sh**ip

z = 'z' as in **z**ebra

ž = 's' as in mea**s**ure

Where a note has a duration of a crotchet or more, the first vowel of a diphthong should last one quaver, regardless of the total length of the note; where less than a crotchet, the first vowel should last one semiquaver.

for those in exile, past and present

Exile Meditations

GABRIEL JACKSON

1.

Pēteris Ērmanis (1893–1969)

Music © Oxford University Press 2019.
Texts by Skujiņa, Zeltiņš, and Dziļleja licensed courtesy of AKKA/LAA;
Darwish texts © 2013 by the Regents of the University of California. Published by the University of California Press;
Tabbab text © Ammar Tabbab. Used by permission.

Duration: 29 mins

Printed in Great Britain

OXFORD UNIVERSITY PRESS, MUSIC DEPARTMENT, GREAT CLARENDON STREET, OXFORD OX2 6DP

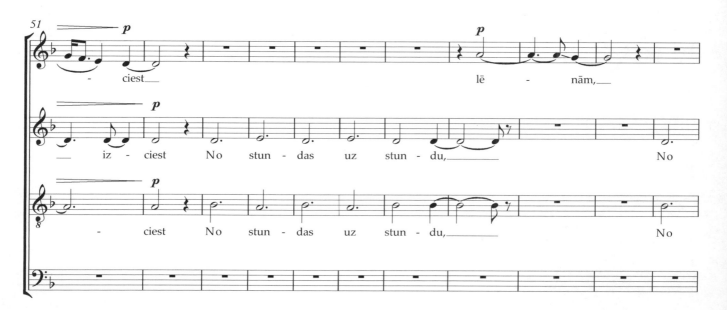

2.

Mahmoud Darwish (1941–2008)

Quite quick ♩ = *c*.84

We journey towards a home not of our flesh.

Its chestnut trees are not of our bones.

Its rocks are not like

The pebbles' eyes are not li-

goats in the mountain hymn. The pebbles' eyes are

-ried on feet torn from roads that led to

-ried on feet torn from roads that led to

-ried on feet torn from roads that led

-ried on feet torn from roads that led

ev-'ry home but our own! The soul must re-cog - nize it -

ev-'ry home but our own! The soul must re-cog - nize it -

to ev-'ry home but our own! The soul must re-cog - nize it -

to ev-'ry home but our own! The soul must re-cog - nize it -

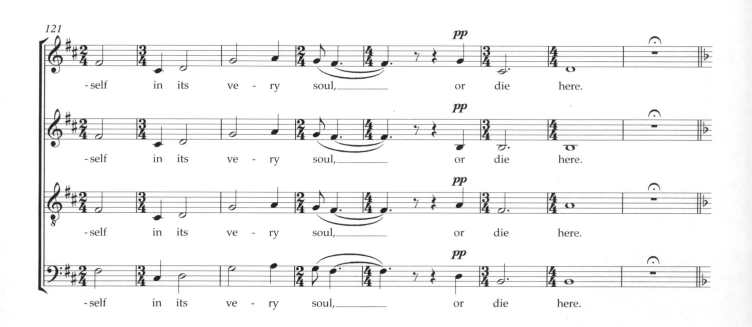

-self in its ve - ry soul, or die here.

-self in its ve - ry soul, or die here.

-self in its ve - ry soul, or die here.

-self in its ve - ry soul, or die here.

3.

Rūta Skujiņa (1907–64)

Me - klē ta - vu ka - - - - - - pu,____

Me-klē ta - vu ka-pu,

Me-klē ta - vu ka-pu,

Me-klē ta - vu ka-pu,

me - klē ta - vu vār - - - - - - du.____

me-klē ta - vu vār-du,

me-klē ta - vu vār-du,

me-klē ta - vu vār-du,

me - klē ta - vu vār - du,____ vār - du,____

me-klē ta-vu vār-du, vār-du,

me-klē ta-vu vār-du, vār-du,

me-klē ta-vu vār-du, vār-du,

4.

Ammar Tabbab (b. 1984)

Very slow ♩ = *c.*52

The night, the night be-came, the night be-came, be-came, the night be-came long,

The night, the night be-came, the night be-came, be-came, the night be-came long,

The night, the night be-came, the night be-came, be-came, the night be-came long,

The night, the night be-came, the night be-came, be-came, the night be-came long,

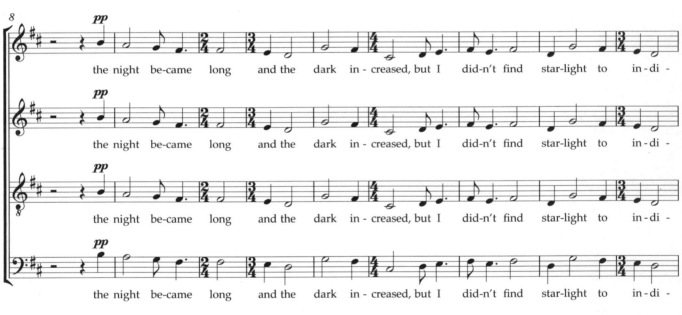

the night be-came long and the dark in-creased, but I did-n't find star-light to in-di -

the night be-came long and the dark in-creased, but I did-n't find star-light to in-di -

the night be-came long and the dark in-creased, but I did-n't find star-light to in-di -

the night be-came long and the dark in-creased, but I did-n't find star-light to in-di -

-cate the path. The trip be-came long, and my foot-steps be-gan to dis-ap - pear, with-

-cate the path. The trip be-came long, and my foot-steps be-gan to dis-ap - pear, with-

-cate the path. The trip be-came long, and my foot-steps be-gan to dis-ap - pear, with-

-cate the path. The trip be-came long, and my foot-steps be-gan to dis-ap - pear, with-

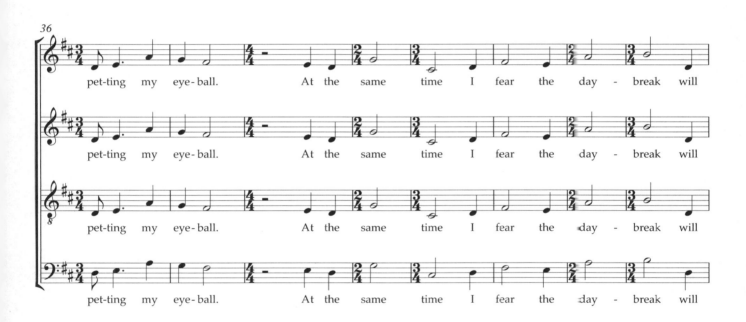

5.

Teodors Zeltiņš (1914–91)

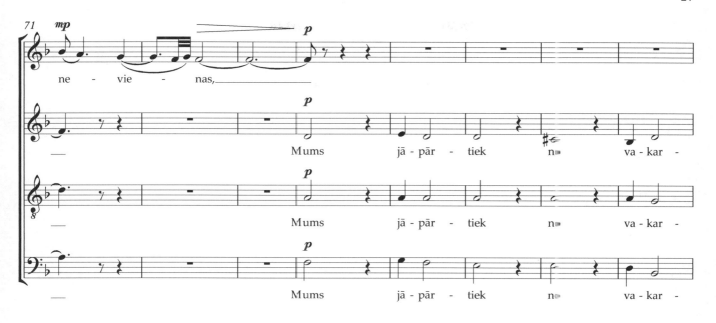

-nas,_____

Tik jā-pār-tiek no va-kar-die-nas.___

Tik jā-pār-tiek no va-kar-die-nas.___

Tik jā-pār-tiek no va-kar-die-nas.___

No ga-da ga-dā_____ rie-ciens plā-nāks,___

No ga-da ga-dā_____ rie-ciens plā-nāks,___

No ga-da ga-dā_____ rie-ciens plā-nāks,___

No ga-da ga-dā_____ rie-ciens plā-nāks,___

Bet au-gu-mā___ aug iz-sal-kums.___ Jau gai-

Bet au-gu-mā___ aug iz-sal-kums.___ Jau gai-

Bet au-gu-mā___ aug iz-sal-kums.___ Jau gai-dām_

Bet au-gu-mā___ aug iz-sal-kums.___ Jau gai-dām_

6.

Mahmoud Darwish

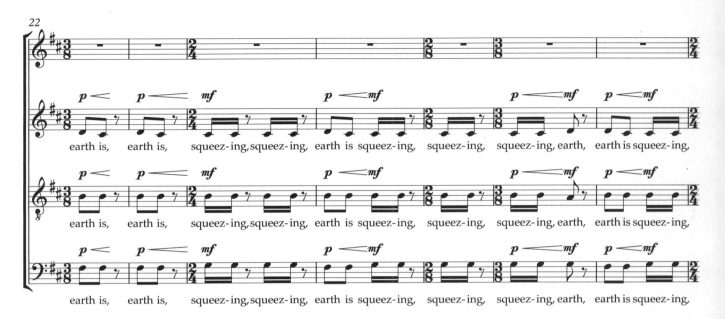

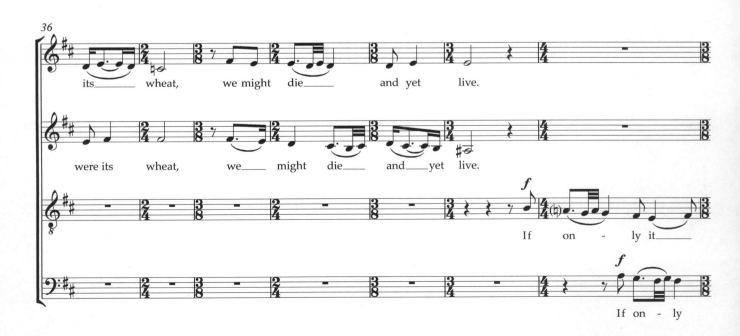

for the soul, of those who will be killed by the last liv-ing a - mong us.

We mourn their child - ren's feast. We saw the fa - ces of those who would throw our

child-ren out of the win-dows of this last space. A star to bur-nish our

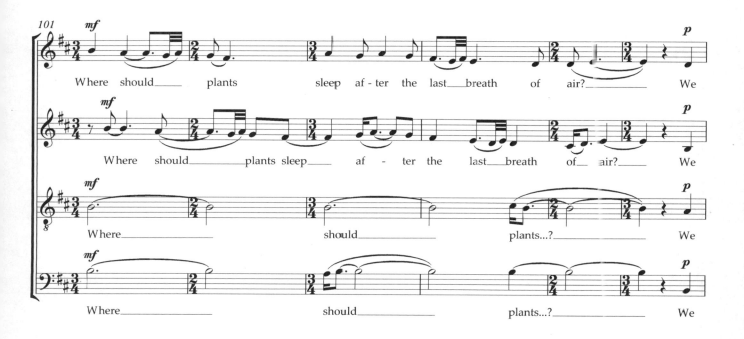

7.

Kārlis Dziļleja (1891–1963)

Slow ♩ = *c*.60

Tur, sa - vā ze - mē, bij man sa - va sē - ta,

Tur, sa - vā ze - mē, bij man sa - va sē - ta,

Tur, sa - vā ze - mē, bij man sa - va sē - ta,

Tur, sa - vā ze - mē, bij man sa - va sē - ta,

To at - stā - ju es bar - gā lik - teń - va - rā, Kaut ma - ni

To at - stā - ju es bar - gā lik - teń - va - rā, Kaut ma - ni

To at - stā - ju es bar - gā lik - teń - va - rā, Kaut ma - ni

To at - stā - ju es bar - gā lik - teń - va - rā, Kaut ma - ni

dē - li gā - ja par to ka - rā— Tā aud - žu

dē - li gā - ja par to ka - rā— Tā aud - žu

dē - li gā - ja par to ka - rā— Tā aud - žu

dē - li gā - ja par to ka - rā— Tā aud - žu

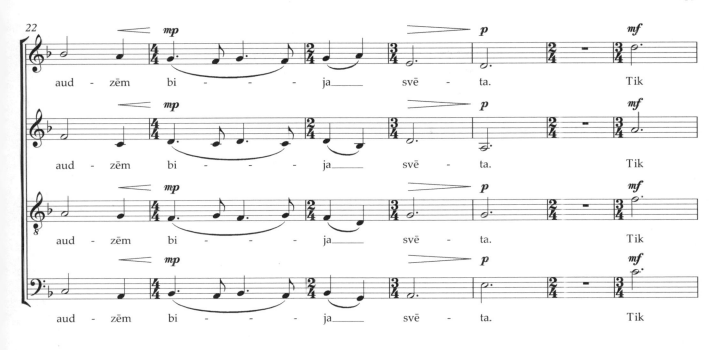

Brockley/Bloomsbury/Guildford, March–June 2017